None But the Lonely Heart
and Other Songs

For High Voice

Peter Ilyitch Tchaikovsky

DOVER PUBLICATIONS, INC.
Mineola, New York

Bibliographical Note

This Dover edition, first published in 2000, is a republication of the music from *Forty
Songs by Peter Ilyitch Tchaikovsky, Edited by James Huneker / For High Voice*, originally
published in The Musicians Library series by Oliver Ditson Company, Philadelphia, 1912.
Contents lists are newly revised.
We are indebted to the Sibley Music Library, Eastman School of Music, for making this
edition available for republication.

International Standard Book Number: 0-486-41093-5

Manufactured in the United States of America
Dover Publications, Inc., 31 East 2nd Street, Mineola, N.Y. 11501

Contents

Op. 6 (from *Six Songs,* 1869)

    2. Speak not, O beloved *(Nicht Worte, Geliebter)*   1

    4. Endless love *(Die Thräne bebt)*   4

    5. Why? *(Warum?)*   8

    6. None but the lonely heart *(Nur wer die Sehnsucht kennt)*   12

Op. 16 (from *Six Songs,* 1872–3)

    1. Cradle song *(Wiegenlied)*   16

    2. Linger yet! *(Warte noch!)*   21

    4. That simple old ballad, O sing me
       (O möchtest du einmal noch singen)   26

    5. What care I? *(Was nun?)*   32

Op. 25 (from *Six Songs,* 1874–5)

    3. Mignon's song *(Mignon's Lied)*   38

    4. The canary *(Der Kanarienvogel)*   45

    6. Some one said unto the fool
       (Einst zum Narren Jemand spricht)   50

Op. 27 (from *Six Songs,* 1875)

    1. To sleep *(An den Schlaf)*   53

    3. Oh, leave me not, friend of mine
       (O geh' nicht von mir, mein Freund)   57

    5. Did my mother give me life
       (Hat die Mutter zu so schwerem Leide)   61

Op. 28 (from *Six Songs,* 1875)

    1. No, whom I love I'll ne'er reveal *(Nein, wen ich liebe)*   66

    3. Wherefore? *(Warum?)*   70

    4. He truly loved me so! *(Er liebte mich so sehr!)*   74

    5. No word from thee *(Kein Wort von dir)*   78

    6. One small word *(Ein einzig Wörtchen)*   81

Op. 38 (from *Six Songs,* 1878)

    1. Don Juan's serenade *(Ständchen des Don Juan)*   85

    2. It was in early days of spring
       (Es war zur ersten Frühlingszeit)   92

    3. At the ball *(Inmitten des Balles)*   97

    6. Pimpinella (Florentine Song)   101

Op. 47 (from *Seven Songs,* 1880)

    6. Whether day dawns *(Ob heller Tag)*   109

    7. Was I not a blade of grass *(War ich nicht ein Halm)*   116

Op. 54 (from *Sixteen Children's Songs,* 1883)

    5. A legend *(Legende)*   123

    8. The cuckoo *(Der Kuckuk)*   127

Op. 57 (from *Six Songs,* 1884)

    5. Death *(Der Tod)*   133

    6. 'T was you alone *(Nur du allein)*   136

Op. 60 (from *Twelve Songs*, 1886)

    3. If you but knew *(Si vous saviez)*   139

    7. Song of the gipsy girl *(Lied der Zigeunerin)*   144

    8. Farewell *(Lebewohl)*   149

    12. A night of stars *(Sternennacht)*   152

Op. 63 (from *Six Songs*, 1887)

    1. Not at once did I yield to love's yearning
       (Nicht sogleich hat mich Liebe erfüllet)   157

    3. Farewell, fond visions! *(Fahrt hin, ihr Träume!)*   161

    6. O my child, in the silence of night
       (O, mein Kind, durch die schweigende Nacht)   164

Op. 65 (from *Six Songs*, 1888)

    1. Serenade *(Sérénade)*   171

    2. Disappointment *(Déception)*   175

    5. Tears *(Les larmes)*   178

Op. 73 (from *Six Songs*, 1893)

    6. Yearning, I wait now alone
       (Weil' ich, wie einstmals, allein)   182

ENGLISH TITLES
arranged alphabetically

At the ball (Op. 38/3)   97
Canary, The (Op. 25/4)   45
Cradle song (Op. 16/1)   16
Cuckoo, The (Op. 54/8)   127
Death (Op. 57/5)   133
Did my mother give me life (Op. 27/5)   61
Disappointment (Op. 65/2)   175
Don Juan's serenade (Op. 38/1)   85
Endless love (Op. 6/4)   4
Farewell (Op. 60/8)   149
Farewell, fond visions! (Op. 63/3)   161
He truly loved me so! (Op. 28/4)   74
If you but knew (Op. 60/3)   139
It was in early days of spring (Op. 38/2)   92
Legend, A (Op. 54/5)   123
Linger yet! (Op. 16/2)   21
Mignon's song (Op. 25/3)   38
Night of stars, A (Op. 60/12)   152
No, whom I love I'll ne'er reveal (Op. 28/1)   66
No word from thee (Op. 28/5)   78
None but the lonely heart (Op. 6/6)   12
Not at once did I yield to love's yearning
     (Op. 63/1)   157
O my child, in the silence of night
     (Op. 63/6)   164
Oh, leave me not, friend of mine (Op. 27/3)   57
One small word (Op. 28/6)   81
Pimpinella (Op. 38/6)   101
Serenade (Op. 65/1)   171
Some one said unto the fool (Op. 25/6)   50
Song of the gipsy girl (Op. 60/7)   144
Speak not, O beloved (Op. 6/2)   1
Tears (Op. 65/5)   178
That simple old ballad, O sing me
     (Op. 16/4)   26
To sleep (Op. 27/1)   53
'T was you alone (Op. 57/6)   136
Was I not a blade of grass (Op. 47/7)   116
What care I? (Op. 16/5)   32
Wherefore? (Op. 28/3)   70
Whether day dawns (Op. 47/6)   109
Why? (Op. 6/5)   8
Yearning, I wait now alone (Op. 73/6)   182

GERMAN AND FRENCH TITLES
arranged alphabetically

An den Schlaf (Op. 27/1)   53
Déception (Op. 65/2)   175
Einst zum Narren Jemand spricht (Op. 25/6)   50
Einzig Wörtchen, Ein (Op. 28/6)   81
Er liebte mich so sehr! (Op. 28/4)   74
Es war zur ersten Frühlingszeit (Op. 38/2)   92
Fahrt hin, ihr Träume! (Op. 63/3)   161
Hat die Mutter zu so schwerem Leide
     (Op. 27/5)   61
Inmitten des Balles (Op. 38/3)   97
Kanarienvogel, Der (Op. 25/4)   45
Kein Wort von dir (Op. 28/5)   78
Kuckuk, Der (Op. 54/8)   127
Larmes, Les (Op. 65/5)   178
Lebewohl (Op. 60/8)   149
Legende (Op. 54/5)   123
Lied der Zigeunerin (Op. 60/7)   144
Mignon's Lied (Op. 25/3)   38
Nein, wen ich liebe (Op. 28/1)   66
Nicht sogleich hat mich Liebe erfüllet
     (Op. 63/1)   157
Nicht Worte, Geliebter (Op. 6/2)   1
Nur du allein (Op. 57/6)   136
Nur wer die Sehnsucht kennt (Op. 6/6)   12
O geh' nicht von mir, mein Freund (Op. 27/3)   57
O, mein Kind, durch die schweigende Nacht
     (Op. 63/6)   164
O möchtest du einmal noch singen (Op. 16/4)   26
Ob heller Tag (Op. 47/6)   109
Pimpinella (Op. 38/6)   101
Sérénade (Op. 65/1)   171
Si vous saviez (Op. 60/3)   139
Ständchen des Don Juan (Op. 38/1)   85
Sternennacht (Op. 60/12)   152
Thräne bebt, Die (Op. 6/4)   4
Tod, Der (Op. 57/5)   133
War ich nicht ein Halm (Op. 47/7)   116
Warte noch! (Op. 16/2)   21
Warum? [Wherefore?] (Op. 28/3)   70
Warum? [Why?] (Op. 6/5)   8
Was nun? (Op. 16/5)   32
Weil' ich, wie einstmals, allein (Op. 73/6)   182
Wiegenlied (Op. 16/1)   16

SPEAK NOT, O BELOVED
(NICHT WORTE, GELIEBTER)

German by Hans Schmidt
from the Russian of PLESCHTSCHEJEW
Translated by Charles Fonteyn Manney

(Composed in 1869)

(Original Key)

PETER ILYITCH TCHAÏKOVSKY, Op. 6, № 2

Andante ma non troppo

PIANO

Speak not, O be-lov-ed, O sigh___ not!
Nicht Wor-te, Ge-lieb-ter! nicht Seuf - zer!

In si-lence meet sor-row im-pend-ing, As mute and a-lone there
So schweig-sam lass wer-den uns Bei - de, wie schwei-gend und ein-sam

a-bove yon-der tomb-stone The tall weep-ing wil-low is
auch ü-ber den Grab-stein sich nei-get die trau-ern-de

2

ENDLESS LOVE
(DIE THRÄNE BEBT)

(Composed in 1869)

(Original Key, Gb)

From the Russian of A. TOLSTOI
Translated by Isabella G. Parker

PETER ILYITCH TCHAÏKOVSKY, Op. 6, № 4

trem - bling tears_____ in thy dear eyes are shin-ing, O weep thou
Thrä - ne bebt_____ im Au - ge der die schwe-re! O wei - ne

WHY?.
(WARUM?)

(Composed in 1869)

(*Original Key*)

German from a Russian version
of a poem by *)HEINRICH HEINE (1799-1856)
Translated by Arthur Westbrook

PETER ILYITCH TCHAÏKOVSKY, Op.6, № 5

Tell me why are the ros - es so pale?
Wa - rum sind denn die Ro - sen so blass?

Dear-est love, how their pure blos-soms fail!
sü - sses Lieb, kannst du sa - gen mir das?

Why so heav - y with
Wa - rum sind denn den

tear drops un-shed
Veil - chen im Gras

Doth the vio - let in - cline her sweet head?
wie von Thrä - nen die Aeu - ge - lein nass?

*)**The retention of Heine's original text is not possible as the composer used a Russian translation in a different metre.**

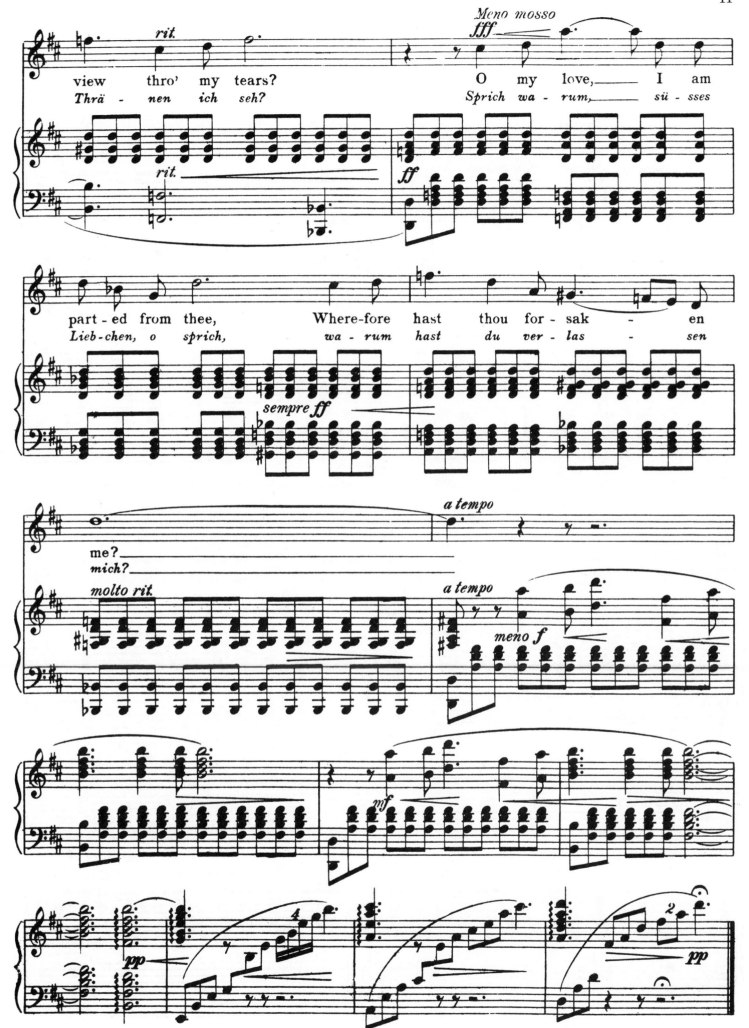

view thro' my tears?   O my love,___ I am
Thrä - nen ich seh?   Sprich wa - rum,___ sü - sses

part - ed from thee,   Where-fore hast thou for - sak - en
Lieb - chen, o sprich,   wa - rum hast du ver - las - sen

me?___
mich?___

NONE BUT THE LONELY HEART
(NUR WER DIE SEHNSUCHT KENNT)

(Composed in 1869)

(Original Key, D♭)

JOHANN WOLFGANG von GOETHE (1749-1882)
Translated by Arthur Westbrook

PETER ILYITCH TCHAÏKOVSKY, Op.6, №6

CRADLE SONG
(WIEGENLIED)

(Composed in 1873)

(Original Key)

German by Ferdinand Gumbert
from the Russian of MAIKOW
Translated by Charles Fonteyn Manney

PETER ILYITCH TCHAÏKOVSKY, Op. 16, №1

Andantino

PIANO

Sleep,   O ba - by mine,   sleep and dream,   ba - by mine!
Schla - fe, Kind - chen, ein;   schla - fe ein,   schla - fe ein!

Peace - ful slum - ber now be thine.
Ru - hig mag dein Schlum - mer sein.

LINGER YET!
(WARTE NOCH!)

(Composed in 1873)

(Original Key)

German by Ferdinand Gumbert
from the Russian of GREKOW
Translated by Arthur Westbrook

PETER ILYITCH TCHAÏKOVSKY, Op. 16, № 2

flies;
flieh'n.

Lin-ger yet!___ lin-ger yet!___ all too soon joy must van - ish,
War-te noch!___ war-te noch!___ im-mer Zeit ist's zum Schei - den,

When the dawn spreads a glow o'er the skies.
wenn im O - sten die Strah-len er - glüh'n.

See re - turn - ing the
Kehrt noch ein - mal die

shel-ter-ing night!
herr - li - che Nacht?

Share the spell which her shad-ows are
Sieh' nur, sieh', theil' mit mir das Ent-

throw-ing,
zü - cken,

While the stars___ still in heav-en are
wie die Hö - - hen mit Ster-nen sich

glow - ing,
schmü - cken,

And the moon _____ sheds her ma - gi - cal
wie so sin - nend der Mond zu uns

light;
lacht!

And a si - lence en - chant - ing is
Wie die Bäu - me ent - schwin - den den

grow - ing,
Bli - cken!

'Neath the trees slow - ly fad - ing from sight.
Tie - fe Stil - le, wo Lie - be nur wacht.

While the
Nur die

stars——— thro' the bran-ches are gleam-ing
Bir- - ken uns flü-sternd um-ge-ben,

In our
wie das

hearts——— love a-lone——— holds sway;
se - li - ge Herz schlägt so hoch;

How the
Ro - sen -

ro - ses with per-fume are stream-ing!
düf - te be - rau-schend ver - schwe - ben.

O my dear,
O mein Freund,

25

THAT SIMPLE OLD BALLAD, O SING ME
(O MÖCHTEST DU EINMAL NOCH SINGEN)

German by Ferdinand Gumbert
from the Russian of PLESCHTSCHEJEW
Translated by Nathan Haskell Dole

(Composed in 1878)

(Original Key)

PETER ILYITCH TCHAÏKOVSKY, Op. 16, № 4

That sim - ple old bal - lad, O sing me,
O möch - test du ein - mal noch sin - gen

As once in the days van-ish'd long,
das Lied aus ver - gan - ge - ner Zeit,

For back to my
o lass' es doch

You sang it with
Du san - gest mit

deep mel - an - chol - - y, With tears in your dark dream - y eyes,
Kum-mer im Her- - zen, mit Thrä-nen im schwär-m'ri-schen Blick,

They roll'd down your cheeks ev - er slow - - ly The
du lä - chel - test wohl un - ter Schmer- - zen. Nicht

notes were so mourn-ful - ly blend - ed, In
wuss - te ich, was dir ge - sche - hen, dein

cresc.

And now, o - ver - whelm'd by my sor - row, I
ver - ste - he die Thrä - nen, den Kum - mer; nun

poco a poco cresc.

glad - ly would slum - ber a - gain,＿＿＿ And peace from its
gieb mei - ner See - le so bang＿＿＿ den sü - ssen, den

f

pa - thos I'd bor - - row!
trö - sten - den Schlum - - mer!

ff *molto rit.* (Meno mosso)

That sim - ple old bal - lad, O sing
O möch - test du ein - mal noch sin -

rit. *f*

31

WHAT CARE I?
(WAS NUN?)

(Composed in 1873)

(Original Key)

German by Ferdinand Gumbert
from the Russian of N. N.
Translated by Nathan Haskell Dole

PETER ILYITCH TCHAÏKOVSKY, Op. 16, № 5

Thy face so an-gel-fair it seems, It
Dein himm-lisch rei-nes An-ge-sicht ver-

haunts me by day and by night;_____ With yearn-ing and burn-ing
folgt mich bei Tag und bei Nacht;_____ Ge-dan-ken und Thrä-nen,

With cru-el and ter-ri-ble dreams;_____ With
sie ha-ben mich e-lend ge-macht,_____ All-

rid - i - cule's mer - ci - less dart;___ What care I? Care I?
La - chen ver - höh - nest du mich!___ Doch was nun? was nun?

Care___ I? Tor - ment me, but love!
was___ nun? Zer - fleisch', doch lieb' mich!

I am thy slave un - to the grave
Dir treu bin ich bis in den Tod,

MIGNON'S SONG
(MIGNON'S LIED)

(Composed in 1875)

German by Ferdinand Gumbert (after GOETHE)
Translated by Charles Fonteyn Manney

(Original Key)

PETER ILYITCH TCHAÏKOVSKY, Op. 25, № 3

Dost know the land____ where-in the cit-rons bloom? Like gold the or-ange gleams in leaf - y gloom; A

Kennst du das Land,____ wo die Ci- tro - nen blüh'n, im dun-keln Laub die Gold-o-ran - gen glüh'n, ein

tempo

know the path a - long the moun - tain steep, Where thro' the
du den Berg und sei - nen Wol - ken - - steg? Das Maul-thier

mist the pa - tient mules do creep: In
sucht im Ne - bel sei - nen Weg, in

cav - erns dwell ____ the dra - gons with their brood, and down the rocks rush-
Höh - len wohnt ____ der Dra - chen al - te Brut, es stürzt der Fels und ____

- es the foam-ing flood. Dost know the land? Dost know it well? 'Tis
____ ü - ber ihn die Fluth: Kennst du den Berg? kennst du ihn wohl? Da-

col-umns bear its walls, The rooms are gay, and splen-did shine the halls. And
Säu-len ruht sein Dach, es glänzt der Saal, es schim-mert das Ge-mach, und

mar - ble stat - ues gaze, and seem to say: "Was fate un-kind,
Mar - mor-bil - der steh'n und seh'n mich an: Was hat man dir,

hap - less child, to thee?" Dost know the house? Dost know it well?
ar - mes Kind, ge-than? Kennst du das Haus? kennst du es wohl?

'Tis there I would with thee, be-lov - - ed, go! Dost
Da - hin möcht' ich mit dir, Ge-lieb - - ter, zieh'n! Kennst

THE CANARY
(DER KANARIENVOGEL)

(Composed in 1875)

(*Original Key*)

German by Ferdinand Gumbert
from the Russian of MEY
Translated by Charles Fonteyn Manney

PETER ILYITCH TCHAÏKOVSKY, Op. 25, № 4

Spoke Zu - lei - ka thus to her ca - na - ry:
Sprach die Sul - ta - nin zum Ka - na - rien - vo - gel:

"Bird - ling, rest thee in our peace - ful pla - ces. Trill thy song, nor
„Vög - lein, ist's nicht hier im Thurm am bes - ten, wenn du zwit - scherst,

vain-ly__fly and flut-ter Toward thy home in air-y__West-ern spa-ces.
sin-gest__vor Zu-lei-ka, wa-rum zie-hest du zum__fer-nen Wes-ten?

Tell me, bird-ling, of these
Sin - ge, Vög-lein, sin-ge

lands so far and for-eign; O'er their dis-tant wonders let me dream and pon - der.
et-was mir vom Wes-ten, sin - ge, Vög-lein, sin-ge mir von fer-nen Or-ten!

robes of rar-er beau-ty?" And the bird made an-swer in his sor-row:
in dem Pracht-ge-wan - de? *Doch das Vög - lein sang als Ant-wort trü - be:*

"Ask me not of that far___ land of free-dom,
"Frag' mich nicht nach je - nem___ fer-nen Lan - de,

Here, where ha - rem walls do___ mock my sad - ness; O - da-lisques may dwell here
wa - rum willst du mei - nen___ Kum-mer se - hen, was ich sin - ge in dem

in___ con-tent-ment, But my song can nev-er wake here to glad-ness!
en - gen Ha - rem, kön - nen O - da - lis - ken nie___ ver - ste - hen!

SOME ONE SAID UNTO THE FOOL
(EINST ZUM NARREN JEMAND SPRICHT)

German by Ferdinand Gumbert
from the Russian of MEY
Translated by Isidora Martinez

(Composed in 1875)

(Original Key, G minor)

PETER ILYITCH TCHAÏKOVSKY, Op. 25, № 6

Some one said un-to the fool, "Go thou not to tav-ern cool Since then all must hear this
Einst zum Nar-ren Je-mand spricht: In die Schen-ke sollst du nicht! Seit dem hö-ren's al - le

rhyme, Drink but wa-ter all the time! Hum-bly bend thee o'er the pool, To the brook-let go to school!"
Leut. Trink nur Was-ser je-der-zeit! Lauf' zum Bach, ver-beug' dich schön, Sollst bei ihm zur Leh-re gehn.

To the brook-let then I went,
Wohl, zum Bäch-lein eilt' ich hin,

Spoke him fair and o'er him bent:
Sprach mit ihm nach mei-nem Sinn:

"Thou art wise, so all men say,
Du bist klug, sagt Je-der mir,

So I bend as low I may;
Drum beug' ich mich tief vor dir;

Tell me where-fore must it be
Sa-ge mir, wie fang' ich's an,

There's no more ca-rouse for me?
Dass ich kein Rausch ha-ben kann,

There's no more ca-rouse for__ me?
Dass ich kein Rausch ha-ben kann?

Dear-est brook-let, whis-per low,   How my grief can
Lie - bes Bäch - lein, sag' ge - scheid,   Wo ver-trink'ich

dim.   p

I drown so? Wouldst that art to me im-part,   Hon-or'd wert thou in my heart!
nun mein Leid? Hast du mich die Kunst ge-lehrt,   Wirst du e - wig hoch ver-ehrt.

mf

mf cresc.   f

But say, brook-let, first of_all,   Left the fool the tav - ern hall?"
A - ber, Bäch - lein, sag' erst dies,   Ob der Narr die Schen-ke_liess!

p cresc.   f

mf

TO SLEEP
(AN DEN SCHLAF)

(Composed in 1875)

(*Original Key, B♭ minor*)

German by Ferdinand Gumbert
from the Russian of OGAREV
Translated by Isidora Martinez

PETER ILYITCH TCHAÏKOVSKY, Op. 27, №1

Now dark-some night the am-ple earth doth cov-er,
Die dun-kle Nacht nun deckt die wei-te Er-de,
The for-est trees are
des Wal-des Bäu-me

mur-m'ring low! And now the long-ing soul toward rest doth hov-er,
rau-schen sacht! Die See-le sehnt sich, dass ihr Ru-he wer-de,
For day hath spent and
es hat der Tag sie

worn it so. I call to Thee, O God, hear my im-
müd' ge-macht. Ich ruf' zu dir, o Gott, er-hör' mein

plor— —ing, Give peace to us; Sa— cred to
Fle— —hen, gieb Frie-den uns: dir sei ge-

Thee the in-fant's sleep,_____ the beg-gar's wretch-ed pal-let, and
weiht des Säng-lings Schlaf,_____ des Bett-lers e-lend La-ger, der

love's_____ mute ag-o-ny of pain!_____
Lie-be still ver-schwieg'-nes Leid!_____

Thou hear'st from wound-ed hearts the cry a-
Du hörst des wun-den Her-zens nächt-lich

scend-ing, Know-est how drear de-spair may seem;_____
Kla-gen, Kennst der Ver-zweif-lung ban-ge Pein,_____

but____ in dream,   Let them find peace,_____ tho' but in
glück - lich sein,   lass' sie im Trau - - me glück-lich

dream!____
sein!____

OH, LEAVE ME NOT, FRIEND OF MINE
(O GEH' NICHT VON MIR, MEIN FREUND)

(Composed in 1875)

(*Original Key*)

From the Russian of FETA
Translated by Frederick H. Martens

PETER ILYITCH TCHAÏKOVSKY, Op. 27, № 3

60

DID MY MOTHER GIVE ME LIFE
(HAT DIE MUTTER ZU SO SCHWEREM LEIDE)

(Composed in 1875)

(Original Key)

From the Russian of MIZKEWITCH
Translated by Frederick H. Martens

PETER ILYITCH TCHAÏKOVSKY, Op. 27, № 5

63

Tempo I.

At my win - dow taps a ra - ven, Who glad
an das Fen - ster hackt ein Ra - be, mir ein

tid - ings car - - ries; For the croak - ing
lie - ber Bo - - te! denn sein Kräch - zen

sa - ble ro - ver Says: "'Twill soon be o - ver."
will mir sa - gen: „sollst nicht lang' mehr kla - gen!"

Did my moth - er give me life To draw each breath in sor - row;
Hat die Mut - ter zu so schwe - rem Lei - de mich ge - bo - ren?

NO, WHOM I LOVE I'LL NE'ER REVEAL
(NEIN, WEN ICH LIEBE)

(Composed in 1875)

(Original Key)

From the Russian of MÜSSET
Translated by Charles Fonteyn Manney

PETER ILYITCH TCHAÏKOVSKY, Op. 28, N? 1

Moderato quasi Andantino
dolce e molto espress.

No, whom I love I'll ne'er reveal by word or to-ken, That name be-loved e'en to my grave I'll keep un-spo-ken.

Nein, wen ich lie-be sollt ihr nim-mer-mehr er-fah-ren, den sü-ssen Na-men bis in's Grab will ich be-wah-ren.

But in my songs you'll find in gen-tle ca-dence flow-ing, *The fire of*
Nur meinen Lie-dern will ich lei-se es er-zäh-len, *wie die-se*

love that in my rav-ish'd eye is glow-ing; *I'll*
glut-er-füll-ten Au-gen-ster-ne quä-len, *wie*

sing that in her slen-der hand my heart is hold-en, *That o'er my life and death she*
ich in ih-re klei-ne Hand mich ganz ge-ge-ben, *und wie sie Her-rin mir ist*

rules with scep-tre gold-en! But ne'er will I be-tray the ach-ing wounds that
ü-ber Tod und Le-ben! *Doch nie ver-rath ich ihr des Her-zens tie-fe*

grieve me:
Wun - - de:

My life is blight - ed; death a -
Sie brennt ge - wal - tig,— und ich

lone can e'er re - lieve me.
geh' an ihr zu Grun - de.

But what her name—
Doch wer sie ist—

I'll ne'er re - veal!
doch wer sie ist—

I love her
Ich lie - be

WHEREFORE?
(WARUM?)
(Composed in 1875)

(Original Key)

From the Russian of MEI
Translated by Charles Fonteyn Manney

PETER ILYITCH TCHAÏKOVSKY, Op.28, Nº 3

Why did you come in
Wa - rum im Trau - me

dreams to me, My ab-sent love, I ne'er for-get: For when I wake my
kamst du nur, du fer-nes Lieb-chen, sag mir das! und da ich aus dem

vis - ions flee, And on my pil-low tears are wet. Ah, leave me!
Schla - fe fuhr, von Thrä-nen war das Kis - sen nass! Ach, lass mich,

leave me! where-fore come___ to me?
lass mich, wa - rum kamst du nur!   molto espress.

The wear - y beau - ty of your eyes,
Die lie - ben mü - den Aeu - ge-lein,

And of your hair the gold - en shine,
der blon - den Lo - cken Son - nen-schein,

Your lips, whose haugh - ty
die stol - zen schö - nen

curve I prize___
Lip - pen dein,

These all in my fond dream were mine!
Du selbst, du warst im Trau - me mein!

Yet with the rays of ear - ly morn All van-ish'd, and with
Doch bei des Ta - ges er - stem Strahl schwand al - les, und mit

heart for - lorn____ I fought the phan-toms that op-press'd.
ban - ger Qual____ hielt schwe-rer Alp das Herz be - drückt!

Why did you come in
Wa - rum im Trau - me

dreams to me, My ab - sent love, I ne'er for - get:
kamst du nur, du fer - nes Lieb - chen, sag mir das!

For when I wake my vis - ions flee, And on my pil - low
Und da ich aus dem Schla - fe fuhr, von Thrä - nen war das

tears are wet. Ah, leave me! leave me! where-fore come____ to
Kis - sen nass; ach lass mich, lass mich, wa - rum kamst____ du

me?
nur?

HE TRULY LOVED ME SO
(ER LIEBTE MICH SO SEHR!)

German by Ferdinand Gumbert
from the Russian of APUKHTIN
Translated by Frederick H. Martens

(Composed in 1875)

(Original Key)

PETER ILYITCH TCHAÏKOVSKY, Op. 28, Nº 4

No,   'twas not
Nein,   nim-mer

love I felt.   Yet,   when I saw him com-ing,   My heart was light and   at the
lieb-te ich!   Und   doch! sah ich ihn kom-men,   ward es   im   Her-zen   mir   so

same time fill'd with woe!   With ro-sy blush-es then my cheeks were sud-den flam-ing;
leicht und ach! so schwer!   Da ist den Wan-gen dann ein plötz-lich Roth er-glom-men;

He tru-ly loved me   so,   he tru-ly loved me so!
er lieb-te mich so   sehr,   er lieb-te mich so sehr!

NO WORD FROM THEE
(KEIN WORT VON DIR)

(Composed in 1875)

(Original Key)

From the Russian of A. TOLSTOI
Translated by Isabella G. Parker

PETER ILYITCH TCHAÏKOVSKY, Op. 28, № 5

No word from thee, of joy or of com -
Kein Wort von dir, der Freu - de o - der

plain - ing,
Kla - ge,
Hath reach'd me yet:
er - reicht mich mehr;
who thee so fond - ly prize,
der dich so heiss ge - liebt,

To him in anx - ious care a - lone re - main - ing Her
es bleibt ihm nur die ei - ne ban - ge Fra - ge, auf

Like wan - d'ring star be -
Gleich wie ein Stern ver -

fore our vis - ion van - ish'd, Like mu - sic breath - ing forth its dy -
lö - schend sinkt her - nie - der, gleich wie im Win - de stirbt ein lei -

- ing tone!
- ser Ton!

ONE SMALL WORD
(EIN EINZIG WÖRTCHEN!)

German by Ferdinand Gumbert
from the Russian of N. N.
Translated by Frederick H. Martens

(Composed in 1875)

(Original Key)

PETER ILYITCH TCHAÏKOVSKY, Op. 28, №6

Andante non troppo

PIANO

p dolce

p con tenerezza

Small head droop-ing, here you stand be-
Tief ge - senkt das Köpf-chen, stehst du

fore me, To my words at - ten - tive, speech-less and blush-ing, Un - sus-
vor mir, mei-nen Wor-ten hor-chend, schwei-gend, er - rö - thet! Ah - nest

pect - ing that your tim - id si - lence, As the mo-ments pass, my ev -'ry hope is
nicht, wie die - ses ban - ge Schwei-gen, die - ser Au - gen - bli - cke Mar-ter fast mich

crush - ing. Hopes that hurt by doubts that tor - ture are suc -
töd - tet! wie des Zwei - fels Qual, der Hoff - nung Qual ich

ceed - ed; I wait your an - swer, maid - en,— but one word's
lei - del Ich harr' des Wor - tes, Mäd - chen!— des Spru - ches

need - ed. For you can give life_ to love, Or, if you will,
harr' ich: bei dir ist des To - des Macht, bei dir ist das

slay it. One small word on - ly say, One small word, say it!
Le - ben. Ein ein - zig Wört - chen sag, ein ein - zig Wört - chen!

Still your glan - ces will not rise to meet mine, Un - re-strain'd your
Senkst die Bli - cke im - mer noch zu Bo - den; un - auf - halt - sam

tears in si - lence are flow - ing. Tears! I won - der what may be your
rol - len nie - der die Thrä - nen. Dei - ne Thrä - nen, wie soll ich sie

mean - ing: Are your words un - spo - ken, deep af - fec - tion show - ing? Or is it but
deu - ten: sind die Spra - che sie der tief - er - reg - ten Lie - be; o - der ist es

DON JUAN'S SERENADE
(STÄNDCHEN DES DON JUAN)

(Composed in 1878)

(Original Key, B minor)

German by Ferdinand Gumbert
from the Russian of A. TOLSTOI
Translated by Isabella G. Parker

PETER ILYITCH TCHAÏKOVSKY, Op. 38, № 1

Allegro non tanto

All Gre - na - da li - eth
Al - pu - cha - riens gold' - ne

Dost thou hear thy plead - ing lov - er?
hat den Frau - en zar - te Händ - chen,

Dost thou see my gleam - ing lance?
Män - nern oft den Tod ge - bracht.

Ah, what songs of love I'll sing thee,
Ro - thes Blut und hei - sse Lie - der

When the eve - ning draw - eth nigh.
sol - len wir die Schö - nen weih'n,

glow - ing, O list to my song!
set - ta, schnell auf den Bal - kon!

IT WAS IN EARLY DAYS OF SPRING
(ES WAR ZUR ERSTEN FRÜHLINGSZEIT)

German by Ferdinand Gumbert
from the Russian of A. TOLSTOI
Translated by Charles Fonteyn Manney

(Composed in 1878)

(Original Key)

PETER ILYITCH TCHAÏKOVSKY, Op. 38. № 2

Allegro moderato
espressivo

It was in days of ear - ly
Es war in zur er - sten Früh-lings -

spring, When ten - der grass was grow - ing, And freed from
zeit, das Gras kaum auf der Wei - de, die Flüs - se

AT THE BALL
(INMITTEN DES BALLES)

(Composed in 1878)

(Original Key, B minor)

German by Ferdinand Gumbert
from the Russian of A. TOLSTOI
Translated by Nathan Haskell Dole

PETER ILYITCH TCHAÏKOVSKY, Op.38, № 3

cresc.

V Thy laugh with its joy-ance, its sad - ness, V E'er rings in my heart since that
V *dein La - chen so hell und so selt - sam* V *ist nicht mehr im Her - zen ver -*

p

night! _____ V When wear-y to sleep I go, V lone - ly,
hallt! _____ V *In nächt - li - chen Stun - den dann,* V *ein - sam,*

espress.

V As mid-night is hov - er - ing near, V Thy haunt-ing eyes still I see V
V *beg' ich mich er - mü - det zur Ruh',* V *dann seh' ich und hö - re dich* V

poco meno mosso *p*

on - ly, V Thy dul-cet voice still do I hear. V And
e - wig, V *und vor mir,' wie da - mals, stehst du.* V *Und*

PIMPINELLA
FLORENTINE SONG
(FLORENTINER LIED)

(Text and Melody written in Florence, 1878)

(*Original Key, G*)

Italian by N. N.
Translated by Nathan Haskell Dole

PETER ILYITCH TCHAÏKOVSKY. Op.38, № 6

Say wouldst thou · learn, O my
Non con - tras - tar___ cogl'

dear - est dear, What___ pas - sion stirs___ my breast;
no - mi - ni, fal - lo per ca - ri - ta!

Know, 'tis a strange and jeal - ous___ fear, Giv - ing my
Non so - no tut - ti gli no - mi - ni Del - la mia

106

WHETHER DAY DAWNS
(OB HELLER TAG)

German by Y. v. Arnold
from the Russian of A. APUCHTIN
Translated by Charles Fonteyn Manney

(Composed in 1881)

(Original Key)

PETER ILYITCH TCHAÏKOVSKY, Op. 47, № 6

Wheth-er day dawns_____ or night shad-ows are fall- -ing,
Ob hel - ler Tag_____ o - der Stil - le der Näch- -te,

Wheth-er I dream or life's pa - geant I see,_____
ob nur ein Traum, ob das Le - ben drängt mich,_____

Ev - 'ry - where fol - lows and fills all my be - -ing_____
All - wärts mir fol - get, mein Sein ganz er - fül - - lend,_____

One thought a - lone, like a ho - ly voice call- -ing,_____
nur ein Ge - dan - ke, der Ruf höh' - rer Mäch- -te:_____

Gone are the griefs ____ that my spir-it have blight ____ ed,
Mit ihm nicht furcht ____ bar Ver-gang'-nes mir schei ____ net,

Love in my heart reigns e - ter - nal-ly; ____
regt doch im Her-zen er-neut Lie-be sich; ____

Cour-age and hope ____ and un-sel-fish de-vo ____ tion,
Glau-be und Hoff ____ nung, be-gei-ster-te Sän ____ ge,

All that for good in my soul is u-nit ____ ed, All is from
was in der See-le sich ho-hes ver-ei ____ net, Al-les durch

ev - er to thee!
stets nur für dich!

WAS I NOT A BLADE OF GRASS IN MEADOW GREEN
(WAR ICH NICHT EIN HALM AUF FRISCHEM WIESENGRUND)

(Composed in 1881)

(Original Key)

German by Y. von Arnold
from the Russian of SURIKOW
Translated by Charles Fonteyn Manney

PETER ILYITCH TCHAÏKOVSKY, Op. 47, № 7

e'er!
sein!

pp

marcato il basso

pp

p

Was I not a lau-rel in the for-est there,___ Grow-ing gai-ly in the
War ich nicht Maasshold-er - bee-ren gleich am Rain?___ Prangt' ich nicht, wie sie, in

p

mf

p

più f _____ *sf*

sun and balm-y air?_____ Yet they have broke the boughs a-sun-der, And
ro-them Glu-then-schein?_____ Doch ka-men sie, den Strauch sie bra-chen, und

mf

p

sf

sf

scour-ges have they made of their plun-der!
aus den Zwei-gen Ru-then sie ma-chen!

p

mf

Was I not my fa-ther's high-est joy and pride,___
*War ich nicht des Va-ters fei-nes Töch-ter-lein?*___

Grow-ing like a flow'r at my dear moth-er's side? Yet
Wuchs als Blum' ich nicht beim lie-ben Müt-ter-lein? Doch

cresc. poco a poco

now they force a bride-wreath up-on me, And a
auf-ge-zwung'-nen Braut-kranz sie wan - - den, und ver-

f cresc.   ff

gray-beard I shrink from has won me, A
hass-tem Grau-bart mich ver-ban - - den, ver-

Ay,   heav-y   is my load of sor - - - - row
Ja,   du magst wohl mir so be - schie- - - - den

e'er!
sein!

marcato il basso

A LEGEND
(LEGENDE)

(Composed in 1883)

(Original Key)

German by Hans Schmidt
from the Russian of PLESCHTSCHEEFF
Translated by Charles Fonteyn Manney

PETER ILYITCH TCHAÏKOVSKY, Op. 54, No. 5

124

"Whence wilt Thou wind Thy gar-land fair?" Their taunt-ing
Was schlingst du nun als Kranz in's Haar?" *rief höh-nend*

voi-ces smote the air. "Leave but for Me the
dann die schlim-me Schaar. *"Liesst ihr mir doch noch*

na-ked thorn!"_____ The Christ re-plied, yet with-out
nach den Dorn!"_____ *das Kind da-rauf sprach oh-ne*

scorn. Then of the thorns, all sharp and bare, They
Zorn. *Und mit den Dor-nen, nackt, ent-laubt, um-*

THE CUCKOO
(DER KUCKUK)
(Composed in 1883)
(Original Key)

Translated by Nathan Haskell Dole

PETER ILYITCH TCHAÏKOVSKY, Op. 54, № 8

"From out the cit - y thou hast flown: Now prith - ee, What word con-
„Da aus der Stadt du gra - de kommst, er - zäh - le, wie re - det

cern - ing us is there in town?" (Once ask'd a cuck - oo
dort man von uns Vo - gel - schaar?“ (So sprach der Ku - ckuk

of a star - ling brown.) "What say they of us? What re - port comes
einst-mals zu dem Staar) „Wie fin - den denn die Stä - dter, nun ich

with thee: Say, of the sing-ing of the night-in-gale? 'Twould en-ter-
wäh-le zum Bei-spiel mal: der Nach-ti-gall Ge-sang? Ich muss ge-

tain me well to hear the tale!" "Well, all the
steh'n, das wüsst' ich gern schon lang!" „Die gan-ze

cit-y - folk he fills with rap-ture When thro' the
Stadt ver-setzt sie in Ent-zü-cken, er-tönt ihr

gar-den floats his plain-tive lay." "The lark, I pray?"
Lied im Gar-ten noch so spät." „Der Ler-che wie?"

129

good-ness thou of me hast heard?" "My sis-ter dear, I'm sor-ry to con-
man da un-ten denn von mir?" *„Da muss ich of - fen, Bru-der, dir be-*

fess it: It is a fact—— of thee none say a word."
ken - nen, *es spricht wahr-haf - tig Nie-mand je von Dir!"*

"If that be true," broke forth the cuck-oo wail-ing, "Then I may wreak a ven-geance that is
„Nun, steht es so," *rief Je - ner drauf im Grim-me,* *„so lass die Städ - ter schwei-gen im-mer-*

sweet: As long as life shall last or strength's a - vail - ing I vow I
zu, *ich selbst,* *so lang' ich ir-gend nur bei Stim-me,* *will re - den*

DEATH
(DER TOD)
(Composed in 1884)
(Original Key)

German by Hans Schmidt
from the Russian
Translated by Isidora Martinez

PETER ILYITCH TCHAÏKOVSKY, Op. 57, № 5

'TWAS YOU ALONE
(NUR DU ALLEIN)
(Composed in 1884)
(Original Key, G)

Translated by Frederick H. Martens

PETER ILYITCH TCHAÏKOVSKY, Op. 57, № 6

'Twas you a - lone e'er felt for me in sor - row, 'Twas
Nur dich al - lein hat stets mein Lied ge - rüh - ret, *nur*

you a - lone who brought me peace and rest, 'Twas you up -
Du hast Ruh' und Frie - den mir ge - bracht, *du hiel - test*

held me e'er, ___ my foot-steps guid - ed, When light from dark - est night my soul would
auf - recht mich, ___ hast mich ge - füh - ret, *da schon das Licht in mir rang mit der*

IF YOU BUT KNEW
(SI VOUS SAVIEZ)
(Composed in 1886)
(Original Key)

French by Paul Collin
from the Russian
Translated by Samuel Richards Gaines

PETER ILYITCH TCHAÏKOVSKY, Op.60, №3

The original Russian text is a translation of verses by Sully-Prudhomme; but the rhythm of the music made it impossible to retain the original French.

Some-times your feet would lead a-long the path - way,_ To where I
De - vant le tris - te seuil de ma de - meu - re,_ Vous pas - se -

dwell, to where I dwell_____ in gloom._____
riez, vous pas - se - riez,_____ par - fois._____

If you but knew the hope my sol - i - ta - ry soul_____ doth cher - ish,
Si vous sa - viez l'es - poir que peut don - ner à l'â - me i - so - lé - e

By your glance, so pure,_____ so true and
Un re - gard où luit_____ la pu - re -

you a - lone my heart is yearn - ing,_____ Ah! could you know! could you know!
*pu - re et dou - ce ma ten - dres - se,*_____ *Peut-ê - tre a-lors,* *sim - ple - ment,*

To me you'd come, at last!_____
vous en - tre - riez, *je* *crois!*_____

SONG OF THE GIPSY GIRL
(LIED DER ZIGEUNERIN)
(Composed in 1886)
(Original Key)

Translated by Frederick H. Martens

PETER ILYITCH TCHAÏKOVSKY, Op. 60, №7

In the brush the flames are leap - ing, Sparks fly up and dis - ap - pear;_____
Dort im Di-ckicht lo-dern Flam - men, Fun - ken sprü - hen und ver - geh'n,_____

No one knows that tryst we're keep - ing On the bridge at part - ing,
Nie - mand sieht wenn wir bei - sam - men auf der Brück' beim Ab - schied

here. ___ When the cold gray dawn is show - ing, To the
steh'n. ___ Graut der Mor - gen, in der Frü - he sind zum

road once more we take; Love, I too must then be go - ing Far from
Auf - bruch wir be - reit, und auch ich, mein Lieb - ster zie - he mit dem

here, when camp we break. ___ Ere we part, tho', tie to - geth - er O'er my
Ta - bor fort so weit. ___ Knü - pfe, eh' von dir ich schei - de, mir das

No one knows that tryst we're keep - ing On the bridge, at part - ing,
Nie - mand sieht wenn wir bei - sam - men auf der Brück' beim Ab - schied

here._____
steh'n._____

FAREWELL
(LEBEWOHL)

(Composed in 1886)

(*Original Key*)

German by G. Löwenthal
from the Russian
Translated by Frederick H. Martens

PETER ILYITCH TCHAÏKOVSKY, Op. 60, №8

Fare - well! For - get their mem - 'ry leav - ing
Leb' wohl! Und den - ke nicht der Ta - ge

Those days of an - ger and of griev - ing,
der Schmach des Zor - nes und der Kla - ge,

Of stream - ing tears, ____ that flow a - new, ____
der Thrä - nen - fluth ____ die täg - lich neu

Re - born each day of jeal - ous rue, re - born of
er - presst von Ei - fer - sucht und Reu', er - presst von

A NIGHT OF STARS
(STERNENNACHT)
(Composed in 1886)
(Original Key)

Translated by Frederick H. Martens

PETER ILYITCH TCHAÏKOVSKY, Op. 60, №12

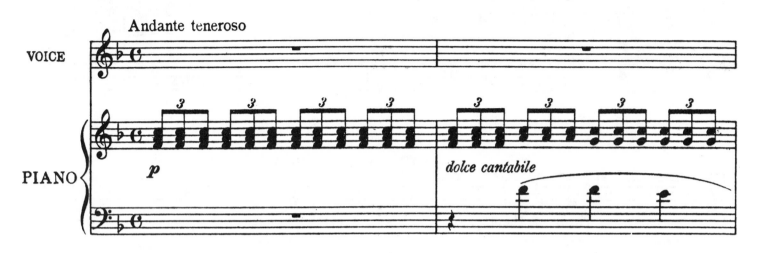

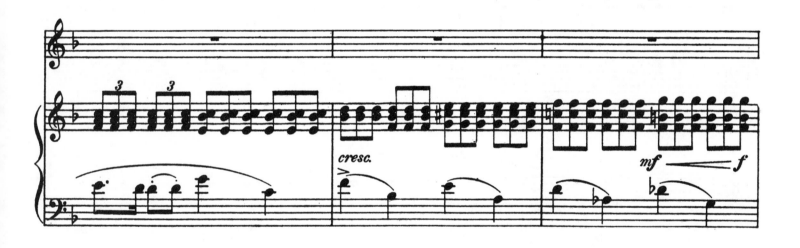

So mild and clear the stars were show - ing, And
So mild und sanft die Ster - ne lausch - ten, es

Gone with your fair dreams love-be-got - ten, The no-ble deeds to you al-lot - ten,
Mit ih-rem Traum von Glück und Lie - ben, von heh-ren Tha - ten, ed-len Trei - ben?

riten.

Our par-a - dise,_____ Our par-a - dise!_____
ein Pa-ra - dies,_____ ein Pa-ra - dies!_____

riten.

Tempo I

The stars have paled that once shone
Der Ster - ne Licht ist langst er -

bright - ly, The flow'rs have long since fad - ed
bli - chen, die Blu - men gin - gen längst zur

NOT AT ONCE DID I YIELD TO LOVE'S YEARNING
(NICHT SOGLEICH HAT MICH LIEBE ERFÜLLET)

(Composed in 1887)

(Original Key)

Grandduke CONSTANTINE of Russia
Translated by Frederick H. Martens

PETER ILYITCH TCHAÏKOVSKY, Op. 63, Nº1

Not at once did I yield to love's yearn-ing, All too
Nicht so - gleich hat mich Lie - be er - fül - let, mei-ne

great were my shy-ness and fear;— With the fu-ture be-yond my dis-cern - ing
Scheu, mei - ne Furcht war zu gross:— Noch lag vor mir die Zu-kunft ver-hül - let,

I am help-less its shad-ows to clear.
noch ver - schlei - ert mein ein - sti - ges Loos.

p

And my doubts and my trem-ors were
Und ver - schwun-den sind Zit - tern und

cresc.

più f

ban-ish'd, At your first kiss they all dis - ap - pear'd,— And for - got-ten, they
Ban-gen. Da zum er - sten Mal du mich ge - küsst,— ist das al - les zer-

fad - ed and van - ish'd, Like the frost when the sun has ap-pear'd.
flos - sen, ver - gan - gen, wie der Reif, wenn die Son - ne ihn grüsst.

espress.

f

Like the
Un - s're

cresc. *mf*

sun too our love has as-cend-ed, Whith-er less-er loves may not as-pire;
Lie-be ging auf wie die Son-ne und sie hat gleich der Son-ne mit Macht.

Fresh____ de-light____ with life's pur-pose is blend-ed,
Neu-____ es Le-____ ben in uns, neu-e Won-ne

Meno mosso   *Tempo I*

And has kin-dled a ho-li-er fire!____
und ein hei-li-ges Feu-er ent-facht!____

FAREWELL, FOND VISIONS!
(FAHRT HIN, IHR TRÄUME!)

(Composed in 1887)

(Original Key)

Translated by Frederick H. Martens

PETER ILYITCH TCHAÏKOVSKY, Op.63, № 8

O MY CHILD, IN THE SILENCE OF NIGHT
(O, MEIN KIND DURCH DIE SCHWEIGENDE NACHT)
SERENADE

(Composed in 1887)

(Original Key)

Translated by Frederick H. Martens

PETER ILYITCH TCHAÏKOVSKY, Op. 63, No 6

166

bee seeks the bloom, So_____ my song to your room Ris-
Fal - ter die Blüth', *mag_____* *mein nächt - li - ches Lied* *schmei -*

- es, round you ca - ress - ing to hov - - er.
- chelnd sanft dich um - flü - stern, *um - schwe - - ben!*

SERENADE
(SÉRÉNADE)
(Composed in 1888)

(Original Key)

ÉDOUARD TURQUETIZ
Translated by Frederick H. Martens

PETER ILYITCH TCHAÏKOVSKY, Op. 65, Nº 1

Whith - er bound, O breeze of morn - - ing,
Où vas-tu, souf-fle d'au - ro - - re,

Hon - ey-sweet, a-stir at dawn - - ing, Breath of day's re - cur-ring round,
vent de miel qui vient d'é - clo - - re, frai-che ha-lei - ne d'un beau jour?

DISAPPOINTMENT
(DÉCEPTION)
(Composed in 1888)
(Original Key, E minor)

PAUL COLLIN
Translated by Alexander Blaess

PETER ILYITCH TCHAÏKOVSKY, Op. 65, Nº 2

While the sun shines in wont - ed
Le so - leil ra - yon - nait en -

splen-dor,   The deep woods   I   fain would be-hold,   Where___   in bliss our
co - re,   J'ai vou - lu   re - voir   les grands bois,   où ____   nous pro - me -

love   we first told 'Mid sweet pled - ges, with faith - ful can-dor.   Thought I with
nions au - tre - fois no - tre a - mour à sa belle au - ro - re.   Je me di -

joy
sais:

"My love I'll meet Be - low the nod-ding beech - tree yon - der,
"Sur le che - min, je la re - trou - ve - rai sans dou - te,

A - gain rove through thick - ets dis - creet, Our hands en-twined in
ma main se ten - dra vers sa main, et nous nous re - met -

si - lent won-der." Yet I seek thee, my love, in vain! I
trons en rou - te." Je re - gar - de par - tout, En vain! J'ap -

call thee! but si - lence mocks my plead-ing. Dark-ness fall - ing o'er
pel - le! Et l'é - cho seul m'é - cou - te! O le pau - vre so -

TEARS
(LES LARMES)
(Composed in 1888)
(*Original Key*)

PAUL COLLIN
Translated by Charles Fonteyn Manney

PETER ILYITCH TCHAÏKOVSKY, Op. 65, Nº5

If you can bring me calm af-ter pain wreaks its pow-er, Or cool the hid-den fe-ver that with-ers and sears, _____ If you but lave my wounds with sweet and heal-ing show-er;

Si vous don-nez le calme a-près tant de se-cous-ses, Si vous cou-vrez d'ou-bli tant de maux dé-ro-bés, _____ Si vous la-vez ma plaie, et si vous é-tes dou-ces,

YEARNING, I WAIT NOW ALONE
WEIL' ICH, WIE EINSTMALS, ALLEIN)

(Composed in 1893)

(Original Key)

D. RATHAUS
Translated by Charles Fonteyn Manney

PETER ILYITCH TCHAÏKOVSKY, Op. 73, № 6

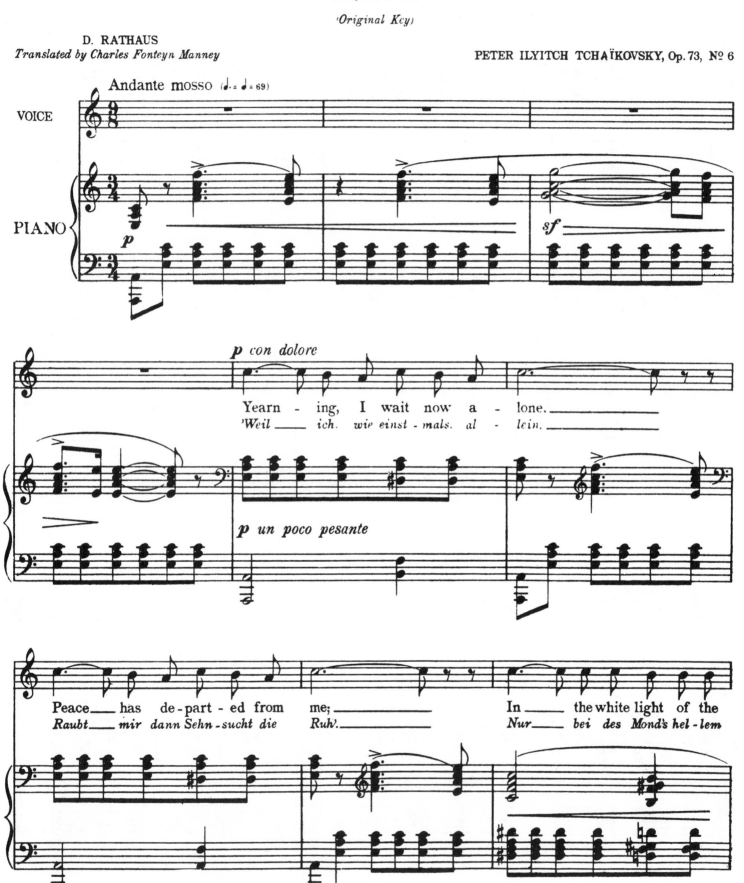